AF590009

GOALS *of* DANCE TECHNIQUE & MOVEMENT

WORKBOOK

N. Brunson

Published by Richter Publishing LLC www.richterpublishing.com

Editors: Brianna Miranda, Austin Hatch, Abigail Bunner, and Lux Figueroa

Book Formatting: Austin Hatch

Book Cover Design: Jessie Alarcon

Book Cover Photo: Firefly Event Photography

ISBN-13: 978-1-954094-99-4 Hardback

DISCLAIMER

DEDICATION

I dedicate this book to the people that have supported me during this process.
Pete, Ruth, Joi, Ed, and Michelle.

Thank you so much for your encouragement and inspiration!

Much love, Ne

NOTE FROM THE AUTHOR

Practice with the guidance of a skilled dance instructor.

Use safe dance practices and ask your teachers for guidance if needed.

Practice in a safe space, that has been cleared and set for movement.

Wear appropriate attire designed for movement.

Table of Contents

INTRODUCTION

Welcome teachers and dancers!

In this book, students will engage in the following:

- Learning some of the goals of dance, technique, and movement. Some goals include: body awareness, control, balance, stretch, flexibility, alignment, strength, dynamics, speed of movement, and musicality.
- Read and write about dance and movement.
- Read and write vocabulary.
- Write about dance and movement observations.
- Practice movement skills and dance vocabulary.
- Create dance and movement.
- Review and assess progress in dance and movement.

Hope you enjoy learning and creating. Happy Dancing!

Goals *of* Dance Technique *&* Movement

Workbook

When dancers learn a movement or a dance, there is a goal. Whether it is to learn the dance, follow movement directions, or apply dance notes, goals are an important part of learning any style of movement. The goals in technique and movement allow movers to develop their skills, practice effectively, and create beautiful dances for the audience to enjoy. The goals of dance, technique, and movement are an essential part of the dance class.

Goals of Dance: Technique and Movement

Review the list of goals of dance for technique and movement.
Write the goals in the space provided below.

GOALS OF DANCE TECHNIQUE AND MOVEMENT	WRITE IT
Body Awareness/Control	______________________
Balance	______________________
Stretch and Flexibility	______________________
Alignment	______________________
Strength	______________________
Dynamics	______________________
Speed in Movement	______________________
Musicality in Movement	______________________

Discuss the goals of dance for technique and movement. Think about the words written above. Why is it important to learn this vocabulary? How do these words relate to your dance class? How do they relate to creating a dance?

Goals of Dance: Technique and Movement Discussion Continued

Activity: Learn a combination, take a class, observe a dance class, or watch a dance. After observing the movement, answer the questions below.

Activity Information

Write the name of the class, movie, or combination observed.

____

____

Where did your observation take place (at home, in class, etc.)?

____

____

Which goals did you observe dancers performing or practicing?
List or discuss the goals practiced below:

____

____

Why are the goals of dance for technique important for the movement learned or observed?

____

____

____

____

Predict what dance would look like without the goals of dance for technique and movement?

____

____

____

____

Predict what dance would look like without stretching? Balance?

____

____

____

____

Word Search: Goals of Dance Technique

Balance	Body Awareness	Energy	Dynamics
Musicality	Alignment	Flexibility	Rhythm
Control	Speed	Stretch	Strength
Practice	Create	Observe	Tempo

S	P	E	E	D	Y	S	W	T	E	M	P	O	D
E	C	I	T	C	A	R	P	C	C	R	S	X	F
S	M	N	V	P	J	Z	S	H	C	P	M	O	L
V	N	A	Q	R	K	I	T	G	O	D	U	B	E
B	O	D	Y	A	W	A	R	E	N	E	S	S	X
C	E	T	Q	C	E	B	E	Z	T	K	I	E	I
D	T	Z	P	E	U	Y	N	A	R	D	C	R	B
S	A	C	B	I	F	G	G	X	O	O	A	V	I
A	E	H	C	T	E	R	T	S	L	R	L	E	L
R	R	G	H	E	B	E	H	F	W	D	I	J	I
A	C	A	L	I	G	N	M	E	N	T	T	I	T
B	A	L	A	N	C	E	U	X	W	E	Y	A	Y
D	Y	N	A	M	I	C	S	R	H	Y	T	H	M

BODY AWARENESS AND CONTROL

Goals of Dance
Body Awareness and Control Checklist

In this lesson, students will:

______ Define body awareness and control.

______ Learn a combination; practice body awareness.

______ Observe movement.

______ Write notes on skills learned.

______ Assess skills learned.

______ Other - Students and teachers can include additional goals below.

____

____

____

Goals of Dance

Introduction to Body Awareness and Control

Being aware of the body and having control is ultimately an artform. If done successfully, this idea can add moments of excitement to the choreography and the performance. Even when the choreography calls for the dancer to perform out of control, the dancer is still in control of their movement. The dancer's awareness of the body is exciting to watch.

Define the words below.

What is **CONTROL?**

____

____

What is **AWARENESS?**

____

____

How do the definitions of **control** and **awareness** relate to dance and movement? Why is this important?

____

____

Goals of Dance
Introduction to Body Awareness and Control Continued

How can you use **movement control** and **body awareness** together in class? How do the two elements work together to help your dancing?

____

____

____

Teachers: Select a dance that shows dancers moving and controlling their bodies. The video can demonstrate any style of movement such as hip hop, ballet, modern dance, contemporary movement, dances of the world, etc.

Discuss the video using the questions in the grey box on the next page.

Name of dance/movie/video observed:

____

____

Write the name of the dance group/company/choreographer:

____

____

Goals of Dance

Introduction to Body Awareness and Control Continued

Using the video selected and observed, teachers will discuss movement control, body awareness, and review safe dance practices.

Why is body awareness important? Can a dancer perform a dance and display movement that is not in control? Can a dancer perform movement that's in and out of control at the same time? What do you think about safe dance practices?
Should they be included in a dance class? Why is this important?

Notes

Goals of Dance: Technique/Practice
Body Awareness, Movement Control

Teachers will create a combination that demonstrates control in movement. Students will learn the combination and write the combination in the box below.

Music for combination (title): ______________________________

Name of the artist/musician: ______________________________

Theme of combination: ______________________________

Body Awareness and Movement Control Combination

Combination Notes

Teachers will discuss the movement details in **body/movement and control** combination. Students will write notes in the space provided below.

Dance Vocabulary Words

Please write the dance vocabulary words used in the combination and define if needed.

Goals of Dance: Technique/Self Practice
Body Awareness, Movement Control

Practice the **body awareness** and **movement control** combination.

STEP 1

Option #1: Videotape your practice with an electronic device, if available, and observe the video.

Option #2: Work with a partner. Your partner will observe the combination and give notes.

STEP 2: Write your notes (things you need to work on) in the box below.

STEP 3: Review the notes written above. Were you able to control your movement? Explain your answer.

____

____

What did you learn from observing your practice or working with your partner?

List **three** notes you will continue to work on and practice:

SKILLS PRACTICE/PERFORMANCE - INDIVIDUAL ASSESSMENT

Name: ______________________________ Date: ________________

Name of the skill or combination: __________________________________

Rate your practice skills or combination in the following categories.
Circle the number or check the box.

CATEGORY	Excellent	Very Good	Average	Needs Work	SCORE
Dancing overall; execution of movement	5	4	3	2	______
Energy in movement	5	4	3	2	______
Applying all the choreographic notes	5	4	3	2	______
FILL IN THE CATEGORY/CREATE YOUR OWN CATEGORY:	5	4	3	2	______

TOTAL SCORE: ______

SCORE RUBRIC

TOTAL SCORE: _____

Circle your total score below

Excellent	Good	Average	Needs Work
20 - 17	16 - 13	12 - 9	8 - Below

Please explain your individual score overall.
Which category was your greatest success? Why?

____

____

____

Which category do you feel needs the most improvement? Why?

____

____

____

What can you do to prepare for the next practice skills assessment?
Explain in detail.

____

____

____

Word Search: Body Awareness

Body	Control	Awareness
Timing	Relax	Tension
Stress	Release	Breathe
Dance	Movement	Expand

D	D	A	N	C	E	O	P	G	A	C	M	T
F	A	J	H	S	E	C	V	W	X	O	F	I
S	S	E	R	T	S	D	A	Z	G	N	E	M
B	O	D	Y	Q	A	R	D	N	X	T	X	I
C	U	D	Y	N	E	X	A	L	E	R	P	N
J	H	W	T	N	L	D	B	U	Q	O	A	G
M	O	V	E	M	E	N	T	D	S	L	N	F
E	X	S	O	B	R	E	A	T	H	E	D	O
W	S	T	E	N	S	I	O	N	R	E	L	A

STRETCH AND FLEXIBILITY

Goals of Dance

Stretch and Flexibility Checklist

In this lesson students will:

________ Define stretch and flexibility.

________ Learn and explore movement;
practice stretch and flexibility.

________ Observe movement,
write notes on skills learned.

________ Create a stretching routine.

________ Assess skills learned.

________ Other - Students and teachers can include additional goals below.

____

____

____

Goals of Dance
Introduction to Stretch and Flexibility

When dancers stretch their body into shapes, they improve their flexibility. Stretching the body increases the range of motion and allows movers to bend and shape the body. When dancers stretch and work on flexibility, the movement performed in the dance is effortless. Stretch and flexibility enhances movement. It is important to stretch before dancing to prevent injury. Finding your way to safely create shapes in the body can be an awesome journey as it contributes to wellness.

Define the word below.

What is **STRETCHING?**

____

____

How does the definition relate to dance and movement?

____

____

____

Why is it important to stretch before a dance class?

____

____

STRETCHING THE BODY

How do we stretch these parts of the body? Write your ideas in the boxes provided.

In dance class we stretch...

Hips

Neck

Legs

Arms and Shoulders

Feet

Torso and Back

Goals of Dance

Introduction to Stretch and Flexibility Continued

Teachers: Select a video demonstrating stretching or review your in-class stretches. Discuss the video and/or stretches using the questions below.

What happens to the body when you stretch? How does stretching support health and wellness in the body? Why is it important to stretch before learning a dance? What are your ideas regarding flexibility? Do you need flexibility in dance?
How do you gain flexibility in dance?

Name of video or class stretch theme (focus):

____

____

____

Notes

____

____

____

____

____

Goals of Dance: Technique/Practice
Stretch and Flexibility Routine

Teachers will create a stretch routine (stretches to help gain flexibility) and give notes on the importance of stretching and safe practices.

Think about adding variety in your stretches before taking notes on pages 34-36. Make sure you add stretches in your routine that include other parts of the body besides the legs.

List each stretch exercise below and take notes for each exercise on the following pages.

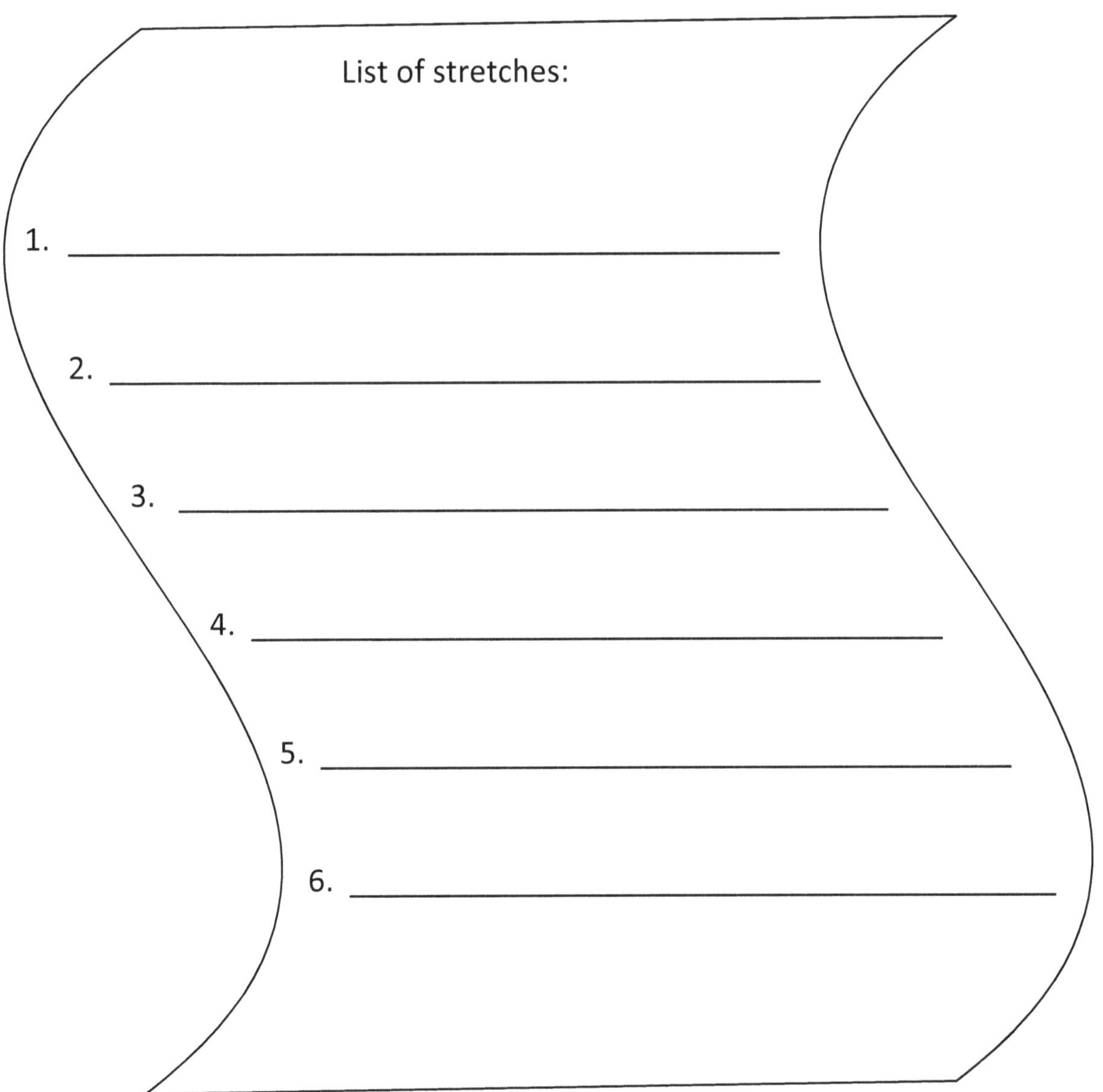

Stretch Routine Exercises for Class

Use the list of stretches (p.33) to complete this activity.

1. Name of Stretch - ____

Exercise in detail

Notes for exercise:

1.

2.

3.

2. Name of Stretch - ____

Exercise in detail

Notes for exercise:

1.

2.

3.

3. Name of Stretch - ______________________________

Exercise in detail

Notes for exercise:

1.

2.

3.

4. Name of Stretch - ______________________________

Exercise in detail

Notes for exercise:

1.

2.

3.

5. Name of Stretch - ____

Exercise in detail

Notes for exercise:

1.

2.

3.

6. Name of Stretch - ____

Exercise in detail

Notes for exercise:

1.

2.

3.

Goals of Dance: Technique/Self Practice
Stretch and Flexibility

Students will select one **stretch and flexibility** exercise from the stretch routine and practice it.

STEP 1

Option #1: Videotape your practice with an electronic device, if available, and observe the video.

Option #2: Work with a partner. Your partner will observe the stretching exercise and give notes.

STEP 2: Write your notes (things you need to work on) in the box below.

STEP 3: Review the notes written in step 2.

What did you learn from reviewing and practicing the stretching exercise you selected?

____

____

How will the exercise you selected to practice for this assignment help you prepare for dance class?

____

____

____

List **three** things you will continue to work on and practice.

____

____

____

____

____

____

____

____

____

Goals of Dance: Technique/Creating a Stretch Routine

Stretch and Flexibility Project

Students will practice, write, and reflect on dance skills learned.
Students will create their stretching exercise routine.

STEP 1: Review the notes from the last stretch assignment.

STEP 2: Select three stretch exercises you want to use in your new stretch routine. Use the notes from the last assignment as a guide if needed.

Write the name of stretches you included in your stretch routine.
Write each exercise in detail.

Exercise #1 ____

Details of the exercise

Exercise #2 ____

Details of the exercise

Exercise #3 ____

Details of the exercise

STEP 3: Practice your stretch routine and exercises.
Videotape your stretch routine. Observe your practice.

STEP 4: What did you learn from observing your stretch routine? Did you follow the notes learned in your teacher's exercises? Did you use safe movement practices?

List **three** things you will continue to work on and practice.

BODY ALIGNMENT

Goals of Dance
Body Alignment Checklist

In this lesson, students will:

______ Define body alignment.

______ Learn elements of body alignment.

______ Observe movement.

______ Write notes on skills learned,
label the body alignment.

______ Create movement; practice body alignment.

______ Assess skills learned.

______ Other - Students and teachers can include
additional goals below.

____

____

____

Goals of Dance

Introduction to Body Alignment in Movement

Creating a lengthened line from head to toe is supported by controlling the alignment of the body. Dancing with energy feels good to the body, but aligning the parts is important for safety and injury prevention. The length and control of the body is spectacular to watch in any class exercise or performance.

Define the word below.

What is **ALIGNMENT?**

____

____

____

How does the definition relate to dance, movement, and the body?

____

____

____

Goals of Dance

Introduction to Body Alignment in Movement Continued

Why is **body alignment** important for dance class?

Teachers will discuss body alignment. Why is it important to practice alignment while dancing? What does dance look like when a dancer loses control of their body alignment? How do alignment and safe dance practices connect to each other?

Notes

Goals of Dance: Technique/Practice
Label the Body Alignment

Teachers and students will discuss the photo and demonstrate the proper control in the body. Students will review the labeled photo showing the correct alignment. Students can write notes near the arrows on the photo.

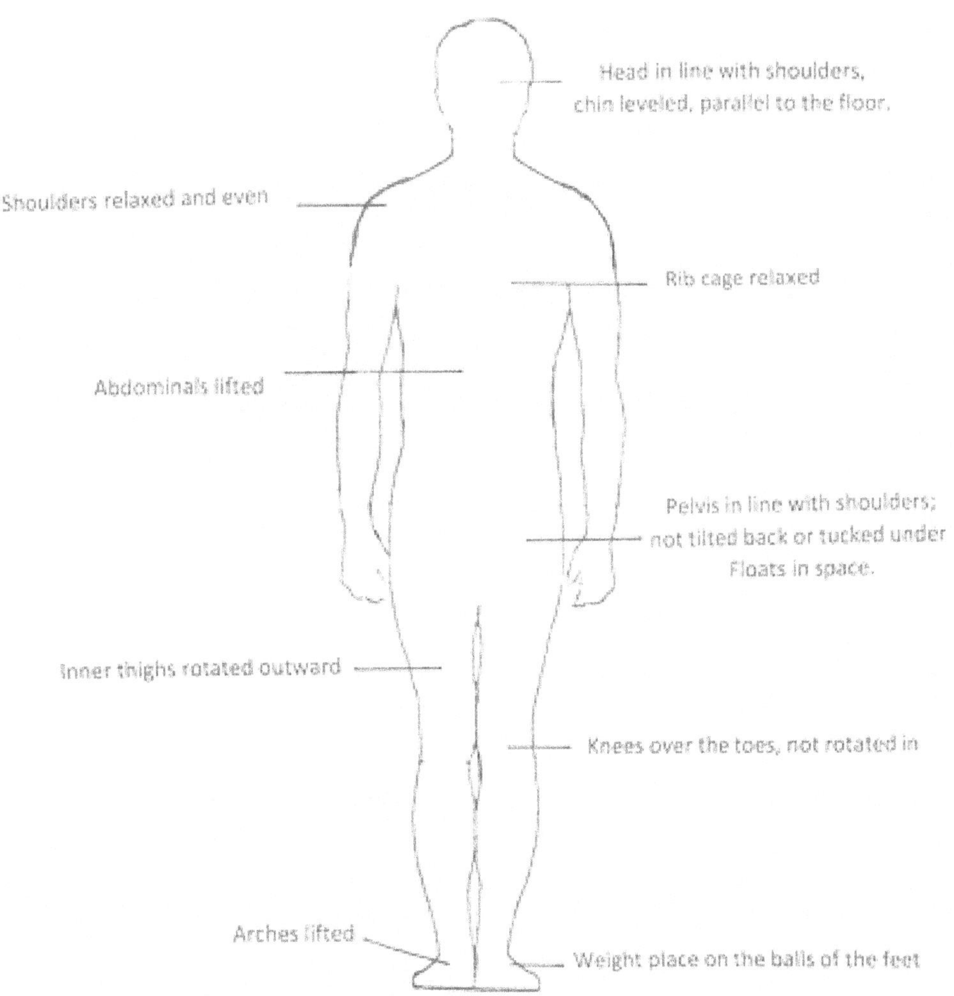

Goals of Dance
List of the Elements of Body Alignment

Head in line with shoulders, chin leveled, parallel to the floor.

Shoulders relaxed and even.

Rib cage relaxed.

Abdominals lifted.

Pelvis in line with shoulders; not tilted back or tucked under.
Floating image in space.

Inner thighs rotated outward.

Knees over the toes, not rotated in.

Arches lifted.

Weight place on the balls of the feet.

Why is body alignment important for dance, movement, choreography, and stretching?

Predict what dance would look like without proper alignment and control.

Goals of Dance: Technique Practice Worksheets

Discussion of Elements of Body Alignment

Students will discuss and write why body alignment is important for dance, movement, stretching, and choreography.

____

____

____

____

____

____

____

____

____

____

Head in line with shoulders, chin leveled, parallel to the floor.

FACTS ABOUT THE ALIGNMENT

- The head is placed even between the shoulders.
- The chin is leveled and not lifted toward the ceiling or lowered toward the earth.
- Movers should feel energy lifting from the top of the head through the ceiling.

Other important information:

____

____

<u>Practice - Write the element</u>

____

<u>Practice - Element of Alignment, Head</u>

Students can practice carefully tipping their head forward, backward, and side-to-side. Then, center the head and level the chin.

<u>Preparing for Technique/Dance Class</u>

How would you use this element to practice dance, movement, and technique?

____

____

List technical dance skills/steps that are important for this element.

____

____

Shoulders relaxed and even.

FACTS ABOUT THE ALIGNMENT

- The shoulders are relaxed and even, if possible.
- The shoulders never shift forward, backward, upwards, nor press down.
- They should be placed in line or right over the hips.
- The shoulders have a lengthening, "away from each other" energy, not coming toward each other.
- The scapula is separated, not pushed together.
- The lengthening allows dancers to relax the shoulders.

Other important information:

____

____

<u>Practice - Write the element</u>

____

<u>Practice - Element of Alignment, Shoulders</u>

Students can practice lifting the shoulders towards the ears. Then relax. Move the shoulders forward, then backward. Then allow the shoulders to relax, placing the shoulders in the correct position.

<u>Preparing for Technique/Dance Class</u>

How would you use this element to practice dance, movement, and technique?

____

____

List technical dance skills/steps that are important for this element.

____

____

Rib cage relaxed.

FACTS ABOUT THE ALIGNMENT

- The rib cage is relaxed or lowered. The image is flat without forcing this action.
- While relaxing the rib cage, the energy continues to lengthen through the spine.
- The relaxing and lengthening actions take place at the same time.
- Do not press, force, or push the rib cage flat.
- Do not hold your breath.

Other important information:

____

____

Practice - Write the element

____

Practice - Element of Alignment, Rib Cage

Students can begin by locating the rib cage. Gently place your hands on the higher part of your belly. Lift the chest toward the ceiling, the rib cage is located near your thumbs. Now relax the torso, lower the chest, and allow the rib cage to relax. Do not press, force, or push the rib cage flat.

Preparing for Technique/Dance Class

How would you use this element to practice dance, movement, and technique?

____

____

List technical dance skills/steps that are important for this element.

____

____

ALIGNMENT ASSESSMENT #1

What did you learn?

Fill in the blanks using the words below.

Shoulders	Rib Cage	Hips/Pelvis
Relaxed	Even	Leveled

1. When practicing alignment, the shoulders are

   _______________ and _______________.

2. The head is placed even between the _______________.

3. Never press or force the _______________ to flatten.

   The image is flat without force to insure safe dance practices.

4. The shoulders are placed in line with the _______________.

5. The chin is _______________ and not lifted toward the ceiling.

Abdominals lifted.

FACTS ABOUT THE ALIGNMENT

- When the dancers move, the abdominals are lifted. This action is created by slightly lifting and pressing the abdominals against the back.
- The lift of the abdominals helps protect the lower back from injury when dancing.
- The lift also helps the dancers maintain control in the torso when moving.

Other important information:

____

____

Practice - Write the element

____

Practice - Element of Alignment, Abdominals:

Students should place their hand on their belly. Allow the belly to expand like a balloon. Then deflate, release the air from your belly (or balloon). This should allow the abdominal to lift, creating the image of connecting the abdominals to the lower back. Students should continue to breathe easy; do not hold the breath or force the lift. Do not force your movement.

Preparing for Technique/Dance Class

How would you use this element to practice dance, movement, and technique?

____

____

List technical dance skills/steps that are important for this element.

____

____

Pelvis (hips) in line with the shoulders; not tilted back or tucked under.

FACTS ABOUT THE ALIGNMENT

- The position of the pelvis is placed under the shoulders; pelvis in line with the shoulders. This also makes it easier to rise onto the balls of the feet.
- The shape of the pelvis is like a bowl.
- The bowl shape (pelvis) moves without tilting back or tucking under. This creates a floating energy when dancing.

Other important information:

____

____

Practice - Write the element

____

Practice - Element of Alignment, Pelvis (Hips):
Students can place hands on their hips. Allow the pelvis to move freely; shift front and shift back. Students can add some bend in the knees if needed. Try to find center- find a balance between tilting the pelvis back and tucking the pelvis under. Students should maintain this placement when practicing dance technique.

Preparing for Technique/Dance Class
How would you use the element to practice dance, movement, and technique?

____

____

List technical dance skills/steps that are important for this element.

____

____

Inner thighs rotated outward.

FACTS ABOUT THE ALIGNMENT

- When practicing dance technique, the inner thighs are rotated outward in all feet positions.
- When the inner thighs are rotated outward, this takes pressure off of the knees.
- Rotating the inner thighs outward allows the knees to remain located over the toes.
- Rotating the inner thighs outward also allows the arches of the feet to lift slightly.
- This action also helps dancers stand up and create length in the body.

Other important information:

____

____

Practice - Write the element

____

Practice - Elements of Alignment, Inner Thighs:

With the feet in parallel position, gently allow the inner thighs to shift towards each other. This movement is small and should only move a few inches. Notice how this movement changed your posture in the upper body. Then, return the inner thighs to the correct position, rotated slightly outward. The knees should be placed over the toes.

Preparing for Technique/Dance Class

How would you use this element to practice dance, movement, and technique?

____

____

List technical dance skills/steps that are important for this element:

____

____

ALIGNMENT ASSESSMENT #2

What did you learn?

True or False

_____ When dancers move, the abdominals are relaxed and released.

_____ When working on alignment, the pelvis does not tip forward or tuck under.

_____ The pelvis has a shape similar to a bowl.

_____ The abdominals are lifted to protect the lower back.

_____ The inner thighs should rotate inward, not outward, when practicing alignment.

Knees over the toes, not rotated inward.

FACTS ABOUT THE ALIGNMENT

- When practicing dance technique, the knees are over the toes in all feet positions parallel and turned out.
- There is a lengthened energy in the legs when dancers bend and straighten the legs.
- The knee should not lock in the position.

Other important information:

____

____

Practice - Write the element

____

Practice - Element of Alignment, Knees over toes:
With the feet in parallel position, gently allow the knees to shift toward each other. This movement is small and should only move a few inches. Notice how this movement changed your upper body. Then, return the knees over the toes, to the correct position.

Preparing for Technique/Dance Class
How would you use the element to practice dance, movement, and technique?

____

____

List technical dance skills/steps that are important for this element:

____

____

Arches of the feet lifted.

FACTS ABOUT THE ALIGNMENT

- The arches are located on the inside of the foot between the ball of the foot and the heel. The arch of the foot should lift slightly when dancing.
- The amount of shifting depends on the height of the arch in the foot. High arch (not on the floor) equals less lift. Lower arch (this part of the foot closer or resting on the floor) equals more lifting.
- Dancers should make sure the weight is placed evenly on the balls of the feet when exploring the arch of the foot.
- When practicing the lifting of the arch of the foot, dancers should not allow the weight to roll onto the outside of the foot.

Other important information:

____

Practice - Write the element

____

Practice - Element of Alignment, Arches of the feet lifted

Standing in parallel position, students should explore the shifting or rolling of the feet, side to side. This movement is small. Determine if you need more lifting of the arch or less. The lifting should not cause pain in the knees or body. Does the shifting of the arch change your body in any way? Observe and discuss below.

Preparing for Technique/Dance Class

How would you use this element to practice dance, movement, and technique?

____

List technical dance skills/steps that are important for this element:

____

____

Weight placed on the balls of the feet.

FACTS ABOUT THE ALIGNMENT

- The weight is placed on the balls of the feet to allow dancers to move, rise, or jump without major shifting in the body.
- The weight is placed on the balls of the feet while some weight is placed on the heel. This allows the dancer to stand without falling forward.
- The toes are relaxed while balanced on the balls of the feet and heel.
- Dancers should balance without leaning forward.
- Dancers should lengthen their energy toward the ceiling.

Other important information:

____

____

<u>Practice - Write the element</u>

____

<u>Practice - Element of Alignment, Weight placed on the balls of the feet</u>

Carefully explore shifting the weight all on the balls of the feet, then all on the heels. Hold onto a chair or wall if needed. Find an even balance between the ball of the foot and the heel.

<u>Preparing for Technique/Dance Class</u>

How would you use the element to practice dance, movement, and technique?

____

____

List technical dance skills/steps that are important for this element:

____

____

ALIGNMENT ASSESSMENT #3

What did you learn?

True or False

_____ When practicing alignment, the knees face inward, not over the toes.

_____ The weight is placed on the heels only, not the balls of the feet.

_____ The arches of the feet are lifted, not relaxed.

_____ The weight is placed evenly on the balls of the feet when exploring the arch of the foot.

_____ The knees should not lock in positions.

Goals of Dance: Practice Review #1

Technique & Body Alignment Practice

Select a style of dance: ______________________________

Name of dance style

Practice one of the following dance vocabulary words or select another word.

Demi Plié Tendu Port de bras Dégagé Relevé

Other ___________________________

Select an element of alignment to practice with the dance vocabulary word selected above:

_____ Head in line with shoulders
_____ Shoulders relaxed
_____ Rib cage relaxed
_____ Abdominals lifted
_____ Inner thighs rotated outward
_____ Knees over the toes
_____ Arches lifted
_____ Weight placed on the balls of the feet
_____ Pelvis (hips) in line with shoulders; not tilted back or tucked under

Practice the vocabulary word using the alignment selected. Write the notes below. Why is the alignment important?

____

____

____

Goals of Dance: Practice Review #2
Technique & Body Alignment Practice

Select a style of dance: ______________________________
Name of dance style

Select vocabulary or name of dance steps used in this dance style. Write them below. Then, circle the vocabulary word you want to use for this assignment.

___________________ ___________________ ___________________

Select an element of alignment to practice with the dance vocabulary word selected above:

_____ Head in line with shoulders
_____ Shoulders relaxed
_____ Rib cage relaxed
_____ Abdominals lifted
_____ Inner thighs rotated outward
_____ Knees over the toes
_____ Arches lifted
_____ Weight placed on the balls of the feet
_____ Pelvis (hips) in line with shoulders; not tilted back or tucked under

Practice the vocabulary word using the alignment selected. Write the notes below. Why is the alignment important?

____

____

____

Goals of Dance: Technique Practice Review
Label the Alignment

Teachers and students will discuss the photo
and demonstrate the proper control in the body.

Students will label the correct alignment.
Students can write notes near the arrows and photo.

Label the blank photo

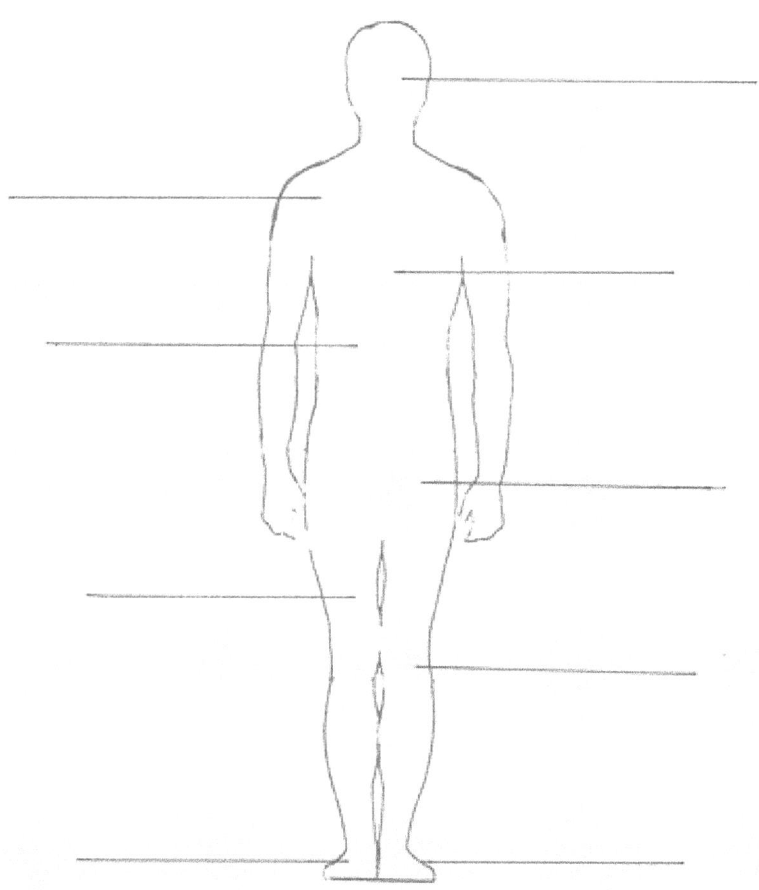

Word Search: Body Alignment

Rib cage	Shoulders	Knees	Alignment
Relaxed	Head	Abdominals	Feet
Pelvis	Energy	Corrections	Arches Hips

I N N E R T H I G H S D V

D E X A L E R P G A C M A

H R J H S E C V W X O F L

S E E R I B C A G E N E I

B D A Y Q P R D N X T X G

C L S D H C S A L E R P N

J U W E N L D B U Q O A M

M O E E M E N T D S L N E

E H S O P E L V I S E D N

K A B D O M I N A L S L T

Goals of Dance: Technique Practice Worksheet
Body Alignment and Skills

Teachers will create a combination that demonstrates control in **body alignment**. Students will learn the combination and write the combination in the box below.

Music for combination: ____

Name of the artist/musician: ____________________________________

Theme of combination: ____

Alignment Skills Combination

Combination Notes

Teachers will discuss movement details in the **body alignment/skills** combination. Students will write notes in the space provided below.

Dance Vocabulary Words

Please write the dance vocabulary words used in the combination and define if needed.

Goals of Dance: Technique/Self Practice
Body Alignment and Skills

Practice the **body alignment and skills** combination.

STEP 1

Option #1: Videotape your practice with an electronic device, if available, and observe the video.

Option #2: Work with a partner. Your partner will observe the combination and give notes.

STEP 2: Write your notes (things you need to work on) in the box below.

STEP 3: Review the notes written above.

Did you use the body alignment learned in your movement combination?

Explain your answer.

____

____

What did you learn from observing your practice or working with your partner?

List **three** notes you will continue to work on and practice:

SKILLS PRACTICE/PERFORMANCE- INDIVIDUAL ASSESSMENT

Name: ______________________________ Date: ______________

Name of the skill or combination: ______________________________

Rate your practice skills or combination in the following categories.
Circle the number or check the box.

CATEGORY	Excellent	Very Good	Average	Needs Work	**SCORE**
Dancing overall; execution of movement	5	4	3	2	______
Energy in movement	5	4	3	2	______
Applying all the choreographic notes	5	4	3	2	______
FILL IN THE CATEGORY/CREATE YOUR OWN CATEGORY:	5	4	3	2	______

TOTAL SCORE: ______

SCORE RUBRIC

TOTAL SCORE _______

Circle your total score below

Excellent	Good	Average	Needs Work
20 - 17	16 - 13	12 - 9	8 - Below

Please explain your individual score overall.
Which category was your greatest success? Why?

____

____

____

Which category do you feel needs the most improvement? Why?

____

____

____

What can you do to prepare for the next practice skills assessment or performance? Explain in detail.

____

____

____

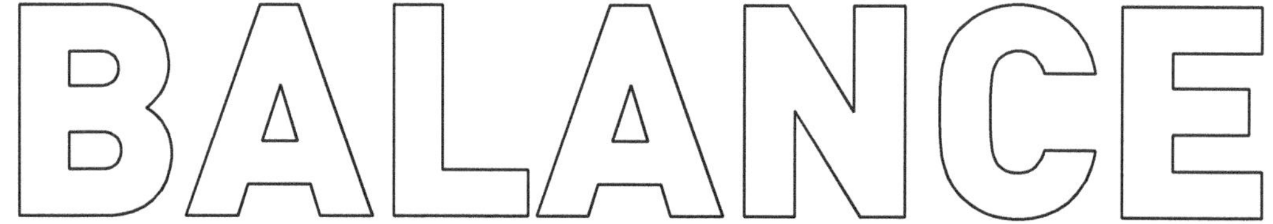
BALANCE

Goals of Dance

Balance Checklist

In this lesson students will:

______ Define balance.

______ Learn a combination; practice balance.

______ Observe movement.

______ Write notes on skills learned.

______ Create movement.

______ Assess skills learned.

______ Other - Students and teachers can include additional goals below.

____

____

____

Goals of Dance
Introduction to Balance

In a dance, balance can be used in many ways. We can use balance in the choreography and when we practice movement skills. When we balance in the dance space, we create symmetry in movement. When the body moves in space, it continues to adapt to the movement, creating balance in dance which is exciting to watch. Whether on one foot, two feet, or with a partner, the action of balance keeps all spectators on the edge of their seats.

Define the word below.

What is **BALANCE?**

____

____

____

How does the definition relate to dance and movement?

____

____

____

Goals of Dance

Introduction to Balance Continued

Why is **balance** important for dance class?

What would dance look like if dancers did not practice or perform balance in movement? How does a dancer achieve balance when standing on two feet? One foot? In relevé or on the balls of the feet? What needs to take place in the body for a dancer to balance?

Notes

Goals of Dance: Technique/Practice

Balance in Movement

Teachers will create a **balance** themed combination.
Students will write the combination in the box below.

Music for combination: ____

Name of the artist/musician: ____________________________________

Theme of combination: ____

Balance Combination

Combination Notes

Teachers will discuss movement details in the **balance** combination. Students will write notes in the space provided below.

Dance Vocabulary Words

Please write the dance vocabulary words used in the combination and define if needed.

Goals of Dance: Technique/Self Practice

Balance in Movement

Practice the **balance** in movement combination.

STEP 1

Option #1: Videotape your practice with an electronic device, if available, and observe the video.

Option #2: Work with a partner. Your partner will observe the combination and give notes.

STEP 2: Write your notes (things you need to work on) in the box below.

STEP 3: Review the notes written in step 2.

Did you achieve your balance? Explain your answer.

What did you learn from observing your practice or working with your partner?

List **three** notes you will continue to work on and practice:

Make a Dance or Phrase of Movement

Create a movement for each letter below.
Write or draw your movement in the box provided.

B	
A	
L	
A	
N	
C	
E	

Put your movements together to create one dance combination.

Practice your combination.

Write notes if needed below.

Dance Skills Practice – Creating a Combination

Students will create, practice, write, and reflect on skills learned.

Create your combination using the skill or vocabulary listed below.
Option: Use the balance combination created on the last page.

Select SKILL/VOCABULARY: ______________________________________

This is dance a: SOLO _____ GROUP _____

STEP 1: Create or develop your combination
(or use the balance combination created on the last page).

STEP 2: Videotape your combination if available.

Option: If you do not have an electronic device, work with a partner.
The partner will observe the combination and help complete STEP 3 if needed.

STEP 3: Write your combination in the box below.
Include details about the movement to help you remember the combination.

Music Information for Combination

OPTIONAL: Select music for your combination. Complete the information below.

Music for combination: ____

Name of the artist/musician: ____________________________________

Theme of combination: ____

STEP 4: Observe/review the combination on video or with your partner.
Write notes (things you need to work on) in the space provided below.

____

____

____

____

____

____

STEP 5: What did you learn from observing your practice or working with your partner?
What will you continue to work on?

____

____

____

____

____

SKILLS PRACTICE/PERFORMANCE- INDIVIDUAL ASSESSMENT

Name: ______________________________ Date: ____________________

Name of the skill or combination: ____________________________________

Rate your skills practice or combination in the following categories.
Circle the number or check the box.

CATEGORY	Excellent	Very Good	Average	Needs Work	SCORE
Dancing overall; execution of movement	5	4	3	2	________
Energy in movement	5	4	3	2	________
Applying all the choreographic notes	5	4	3	2	________
FILL IN THE CATEGORY/CREATE YOUR OWN CATEGORY:	5	4	3	2	________

TOTAL SCORE: ________

SCORE RUBRIC

TOTAL SCORE ______

Circle your total score below

Excellent	Good	Average	Needs Work
20 - 17	16 - 13	12 - 9	8 - Below

Please explain your individual score overall.
Which category was your greatest success? Why?

____

____

____

Which category do you feel needs the most improvement? Why?

____

____

____

What can you do to prepare for the next skills practice or performance?
Explain in detail.

____

____

____

STRENGTH IN MOVEMENT

Goals of Dance
Strength in Movement Checklist

In this lesson students will:

_____ Define the word strength.

_____ Learn and review safe movement practices.

_____ Observe movement.

_____ Write notes on skills learned.

_____ Create strength exercises; practice body alignment.

_____ Assess skills learned.

_____ Other - Students and teachers can include additional goals below.

____

____

____

Goals of Dance
Introduction to Strength in Movement

Exercises that support and enhance strength are essential for a dancer. There are many muscles in the body. These muscles can be found from the top of the head to the bottom of the feet. When the muscles are used in the body, they create muscle tension and contract. Strength in dance increases endurance. It also adds control and stability in the body when moving. Strength while dancing and moving is used throughout the dance class, beginning to the end.

Define the word below.

What is **STRENGTH?**

____

____

____

How does the definition relate to dance and movement?

____

____

____

Goals of Dance

Introduction to Strength in Movement Continued

Why is **strength** important for a dance class?

____

____

____

Teachers: Select a dance video demonstrating strength or review your in-class strengthening exercises. Discuss the video or strength exercises using the questions below.

How does strength exercise support health and wellness in the body? Why is it important to be strong while learning dance and movement? Do you need strength in dance? What are your ideas regarding strength and flexibility? How do you gain strength in dance?

Notes

____

____

____

____

READING:
Common Strength Exercise
Arm Circles, Seated

The starting position for this exercise is seated with legs extended in parallel or knees bent, legs crossed.

The body is elongated with the shoulders placed over the hips.

The arms are placed at the side of the body, relaxed elbows and shoulders.

The chin is parallel to the ground. The torso does not move.

The arms extend to the side, create the letter "T".

Begin making a circle by moving the arms toward the front, the movement coming from the shoulders and back.

Repeat a couple of times, then reverse the circle.

Maintain the alignment of the torso, head, and pelvis when reversing the movement.

Other important information:

____

____

____

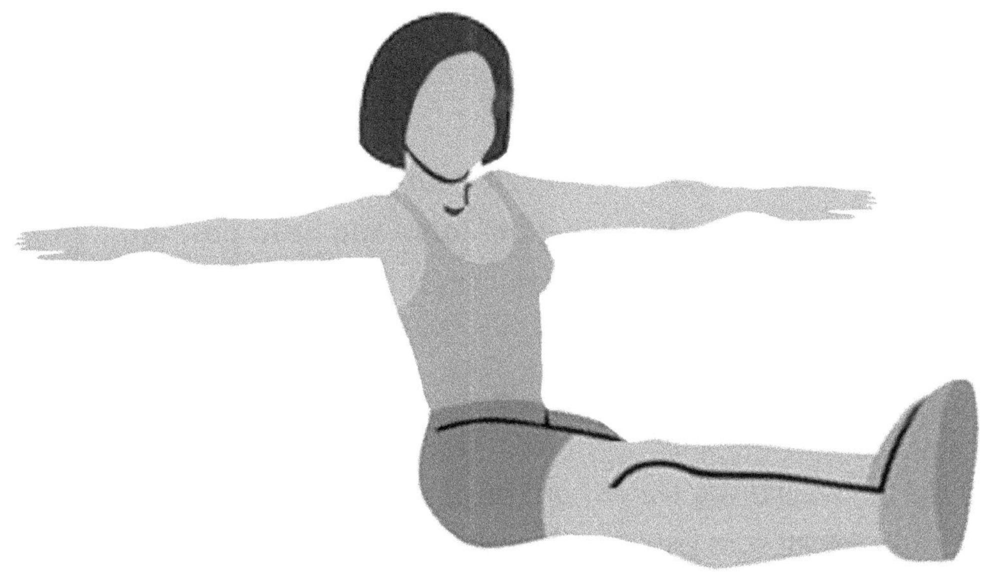

READING:
Common Strength Exercise
Plank Exercise #1 with Modification

The starting position for plank exercise #1 is on the hands and knees with the pelvis in line with the knees and the shoulders in line with the wrist. Do not add pressure to the wrist.

The head and torso make one line by placing the face toward the mat. Lift the abdominals against the back.

Gently crawl forward onto the elbows, making sure the elbows are in line with the shoulders, while maintaining the torso and head position. The knees and feet remain attached to the floor.

Relax the shoulders.

Option: Lift the knees, placing weight on the balls of the feet, extending the legs. Make sure you maintain the body alignment

Breathe while holding the position and relaxing the shoulders.

Slowly, release the body and relax the torso on the floor.

Other important information:

____

____

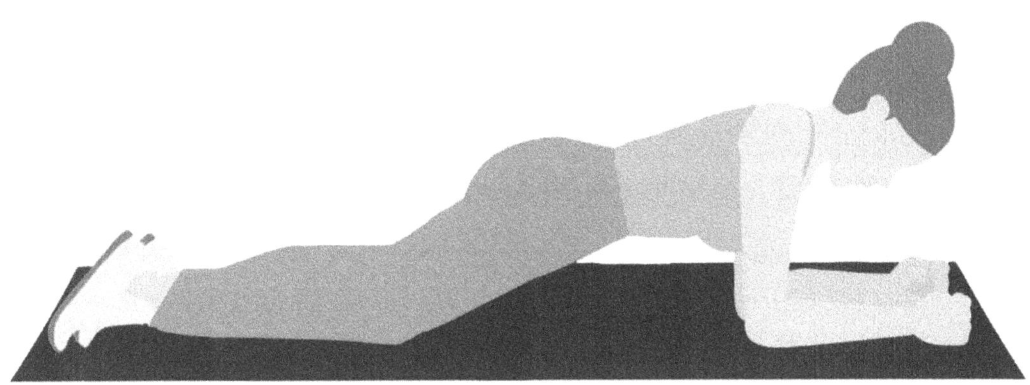

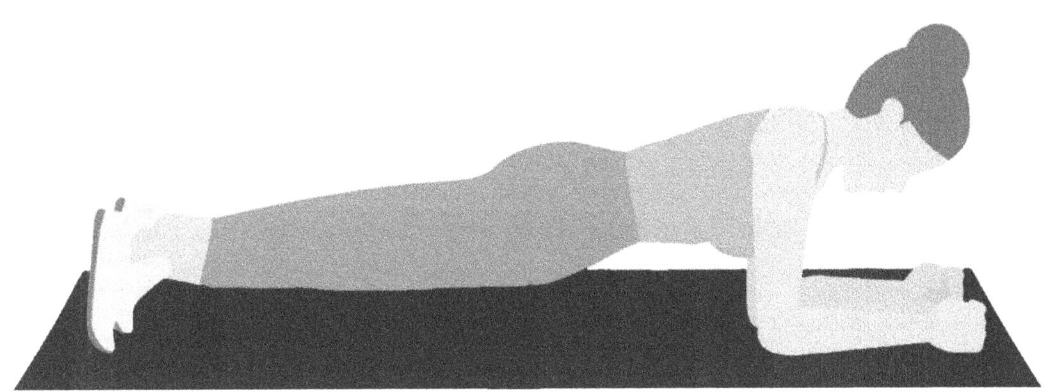

READING:
Common Strength Exercise
Plank Exercise #2

The starting position for plank exercise #2 is on hands and knees with the pelvis in line with the knees and the shoulders in line with the wrist. Do not add pressure to the wrist.

The head and torso make one line by placing the face towards the mat.
Lift the abdominals against the back.

Gently crawl forward, onto the hands and knees, making sure the shoulders are in line with the wrist, while maintaining the torso and head position.

Slowly, extend one foot at a time, back onto the balls of the feet.
The feet should have a small space in between and be parallel to each other.

Relax the shoulders.

OPTION: Lower the elbows and knees if you are feeling any tension or challenges in the position. Make sure you maintain the body alignment.

Breathe while holding the position and relaxing the shoulders.

Slowly, release the body, bend the knees if needed,
and relax the torso on the floor.

Other important information:

____

____

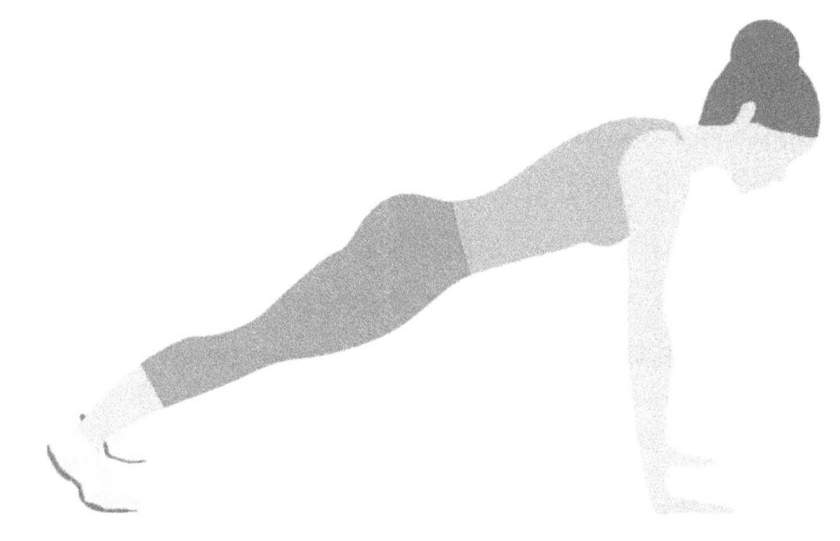

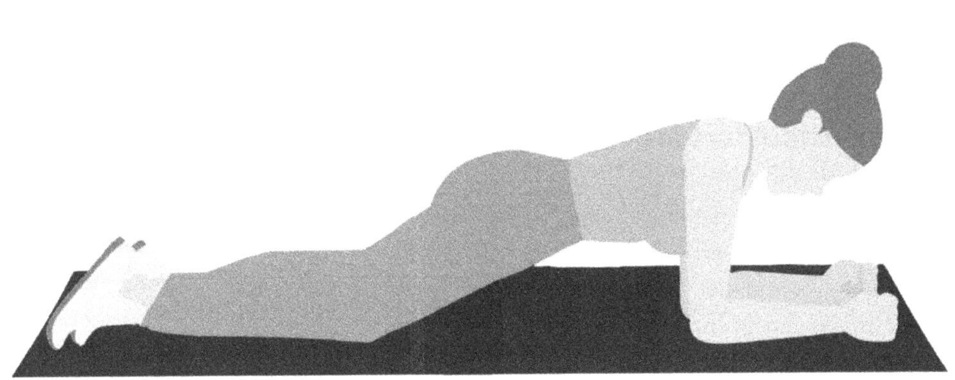

READING:
Common Strength Exercise
Leg Lifts and Leg Circles

The starting position for leg lifts and circles is on the side of the body, bending the knees in a right angle. The shoulders are relaxed and in line with each other. The pelvis is also in line with the torso.

Make a pillow with your arm or support the head and neck with your hand. Extend the top leg underneath the pelvis.

Exercise 1 - Leg Lifts:
Slowly lift the leg toward the ceiling a few inches, then return to the starting position. Repeat as needed.
Exercise 2 - Leg Circles:
Slowly move the leg to the front to begin making a small circle. Make a few rotations.

The body is elongated with the shoulders placed over the hips.

The arm facing the ceiling is placed in front of the body to help with the balance.

The shoulders are relaxed, and the torso does not move.

Other important information:

____

____

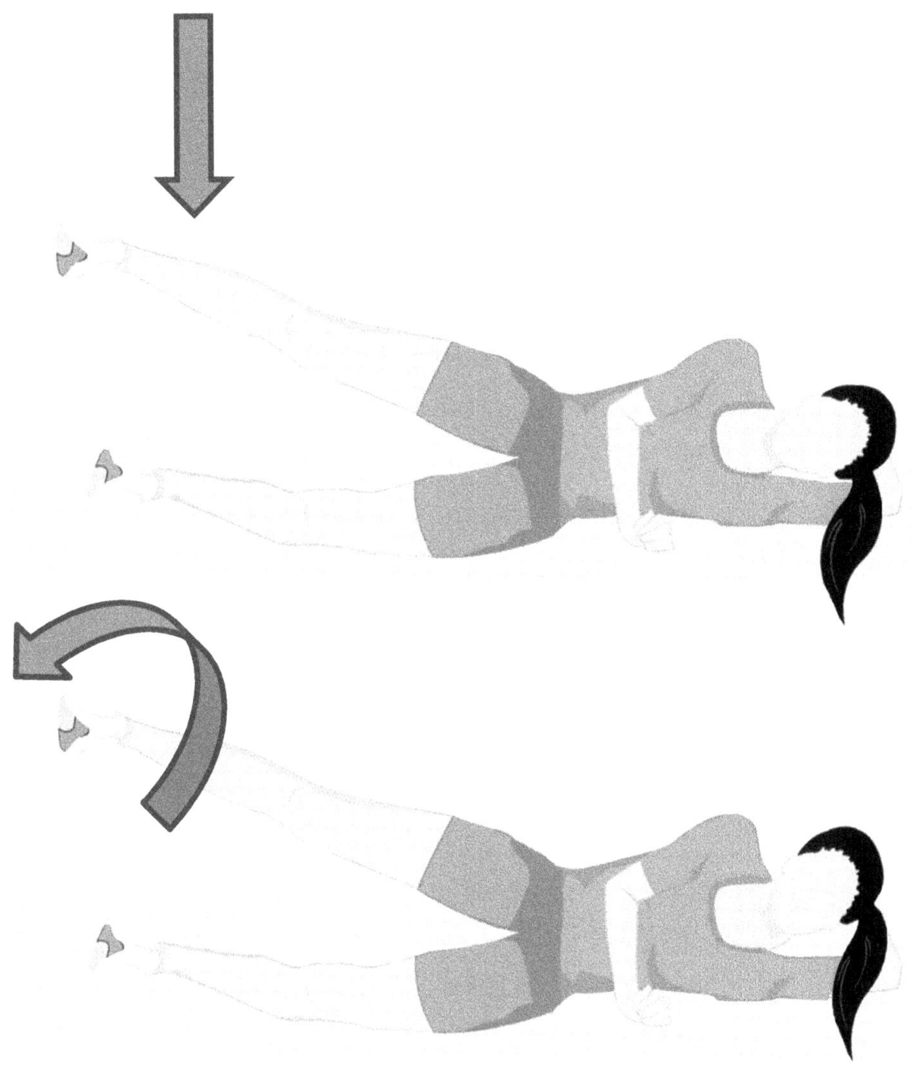

READING:
Common Strength Exercise
Relevé or Heel Lifts, Standing

The starting position for relevé, heel lifts, is a standing, parallel position.
The energy in the torso is lifted and elongated.
The shoulders are relaxed and the chin is parallel to the floor.

The arms are placed at the side of the body, hands on the hips
or on a chair/wall to help with the balance.

Rise slowly onto the balls of the feet, releasing the heels off the floor.
The heels remain close together;
some space may appear between the heels.

While on the balls of the feet,
the toes relax and connect to the floor.
The balance takes place on the balls of the feet, not the toes.

The knees are lengthened, not locked.
The heels slowly return to the ground together;
returning to the starting position.

Repeat the exercise.

Other important information:

____

____

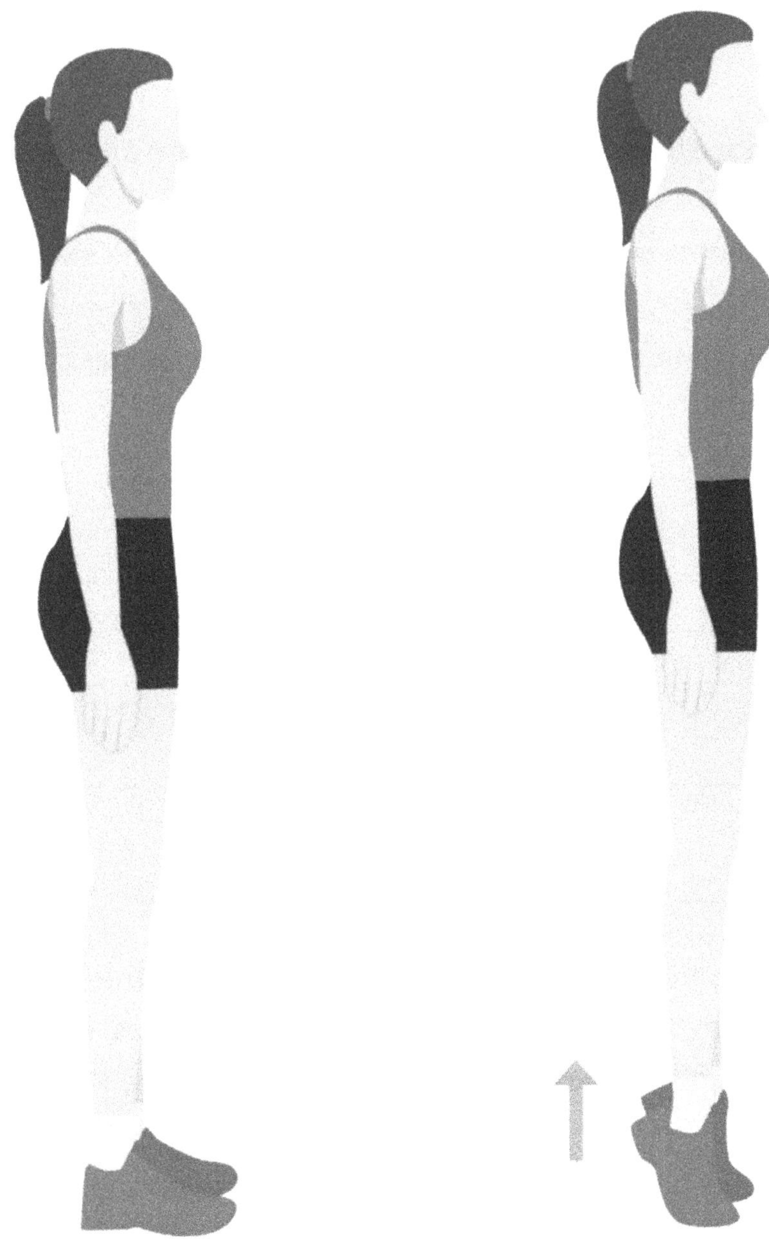

Common Exercises for Strength Practice

*Teacher's Choice

Discuss the common strength exercises used in your dance and movement classes.

Share photos or carefully demonstrate some of the exercises.

List the common strength exercises used in your class below:

1. ______________________________
2. ______________________________
3. ______________________________
4. ______________________________

Practice the correct positions. The goal is to create a strength training routine at the end of this lesson (exercises to help you gain strength). Teachers will give notes on the importance of the strength training exercises and safe practices.

Students will take notes on each strength training exercise on the worksheets provided.

Strength Exercise:

____

____

Primary Body Part:

____

____

List important details for practicing the exercise:

____

____

____

____

____

____

____

____

Strength Exercise:

____

____

Primary Body Part:

____

____

List important details for practicing the exercise:

____

____

____

____

____

____

____

____

Strength Exercise:

____

____

Primary Body Part:

____

____

List important details for practicing the exercise:

____

____

____

____

____

____

____

____

Strength Exercise:

____

____

Primary Body Part:

____

____

List important details for practicing the exercise:

____

____

____

____

____

____

____

____

Name: ________________________________ Date: ___________

Strength Training Exercise Routine Checklist

Name of the exercise	Number of Minutes/Reps DAY 1	Number of Minutes/Reps DAY 2	Number of Minutes/Reps DAY 3	Number of Minutes/Reps DAY 4

Compare the days. What was your most productive strength training day? Why?

____

____

Name your favorite exercise. ____

Why is this your favorite? ____

____

SPEED OF MOVEMENT

Goals of Dance
Speed of Movement Checklist

In this lesson students will:

_____ Define the word speed.

_____ Learn the elements of speed.

_____ Observe movement.

_____ Write notes on skills learned.

_____ Create movement; practice skills learned.

_____ Assess skills learned.

_____ Other – Students and teachers can include additional goals below.

____

____

____

Goals of Dance
Introduction to Speed of Movement Worksheet

Watching dancers perform to different tempos in a dance is a joy to observe. The tempo relates to the speed of the dance and movement. When we add the element of speed to the choreography it is exciting to watch because it helps the dancers tell the story. Adding a variety of the speed to the dance keeps the audience engaged in the performance. Some of the speeds in movement include fast, slow, or moderate speed.

Define the word below.

What is **SPEED**?

____

____

____

How does the definition relate to dance and movement?

____

____

____

SPEED:

SLOW

MOVEMENT

Goals of Dance: Technique/Practice
Slow Speed in Movement

Teachers will create a combination that has a **slow** movement speed.
Students will write the combination in the box below.

Music for combination: ______________________________

Name of the artist/musician: ______________________________

Theme of combination: ______________________________

Speed - Slow Combination

Combination Notes

Teachers will discuss movement details in the **slow movement** combination. Students will write notes in the space provided below.

Dance Vocabulary Words

Please write the dance vocabulary words used in the combination and define if needed.

If I were a dance costume ...

Draw a dance costume for the slow speed themed combination below.

Describe your dance costume. How does the color of your costume enhance the performance of the combination?

I selected these colors because...

____

____

____

I like this style of dance costume because...

____

____

____

My costume is special because...

____

____

____

SPEED: FAST MOVEMENT

Goals of Dance: Technique/Practice
Fast Speed in Movement

Teachers will create a combination that has a **fast** movement speed. Students will write the combination in the box below.

Music for combination: ____

Name of the artist/musician: _______________________________________

Theme of combination: ____

Speed - Fast Combination

Combination Notes

Teachers will discuss movement details in the **fast movement** combination. Students will write notes in the space provided below.

Dance Vocabulary Words

Please write the dance vocabulary words used in the combination and define if needed.

WRITING: SPEED of Movement Poem

Students will write an acrostic poem and create movement on the next page.
The theme of this poem is speed in movement and choreography.

S

P

E

E

D

CREATE: SPEED of Movement Dance

Make a dance.

Create a movement for each line of the poem written on the last page and connect the movement. Describe each movement below in the space provided.

Select the speed of your movement: ___________________________

S

P

E

E

D

SKILLS PRACTICE/PERFORMANCE- INDIVIDUAL ASSESSMENT

Name: ________________________________ Date: __________________

Name of the skill or combination: ______________________________________

Rate your skills practice or combination in the following categories.
Circle the number or check the box.

CATEGORY	Excellent	Very Good	Average	Needs Work	SCORE
Dancing overall; execution of movement	5	4	3	2	________
Energy in movement	5	4	3	2	________
Applying all the choreographic notes	5	4	3	2	________
FILL IN THE CATEGORY/CREATE YOUR OWN CATEGORY:	5	4	3	2	________

TOTAL SCORE: ______

SCORE RUBRIC

TOTAL SCORE ______

Circle your total score below

Excellent	Good	Average	Needs Work
20 - 17	16 - 13	12 - 9	8 - Below

Please explain your individual score overall.
Which category was your greatest success? Why?

___

___

___

Which category do you feel needs the most improvement? Why?

___

___

___

What can you do to prepare for the next skills practice or performance?
Explain in detail.

___

___

___

Word Search: Speed and Dynamics

Tempo	Fast	Lines	Circle	Shape Create
Speed	Slow	Control	Explore	Sharp
Dynamics	Suspend	Collapse	Percussive	Moderate

J	M	W	O	L	S	H	A	P	E	S	V	E
C	O	N	T	R	O	L	P	V	X	C	C	S
I	D	K	E	T	F	C	I	T	P	I	F	P
Z	E	G	M	I	B	S	A	H	L	M	E	A
F	R	B	P	Q	S	U	P	N	O	A	X	L
D	A	S	O	U	C	S	A	E	R	N	S	L
J	T	S	C	Q	W	P	X	U	E	Y	E	O
Q	E	R	T	C	R	E	A	T	E	D	N	C
R	E	H	S	O	P	N	I	S	E	D	I	W
P	S	H	A	R	P	D	C	I	R	C	L	E

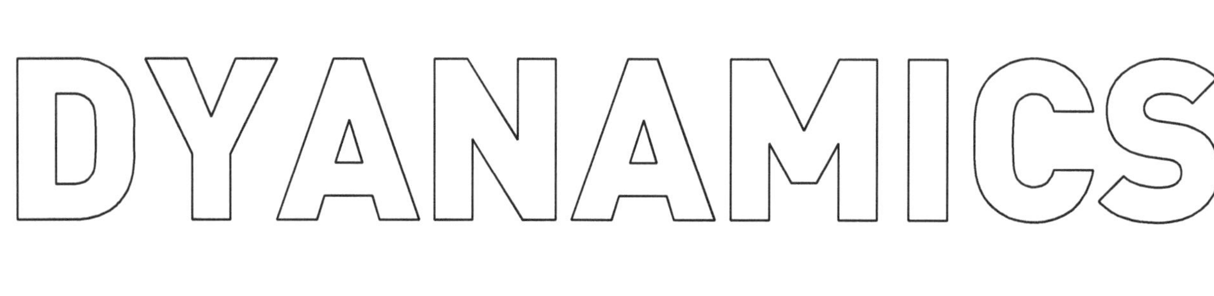
DYANAMICS

Goals of Dance
Dynamics in Movement Checklist

In this lesson students will:

_____ Define the word dynamics.

_____ Learn the elements of dynamics.

_____ Observe movement.

_____ Write notes on skills learned.

_____ Create movement; practice different dynamics.

_____ Assess skills learned.

_____ Other - Students and teachers can include additional goals below.

____

____

____

Goals of Dance
Introduction to Dynamics

Performing with different energies in movement is a great way to express dynamics. The dynamics in movement add life to the dance or combination. Some dynamic changes in the dance or movement can be suspended, percussive, smooth, or collapsed, giving into gravity. Dynamics in movement make the choreography exciting to perform and breathtaking for the audience members to view.

Define the word below.

What is **DYNAMICS?**

____

____

How does the definition relate to dance and movement?

____

____

____

What would a dance look like without dynamics?

____

____

____

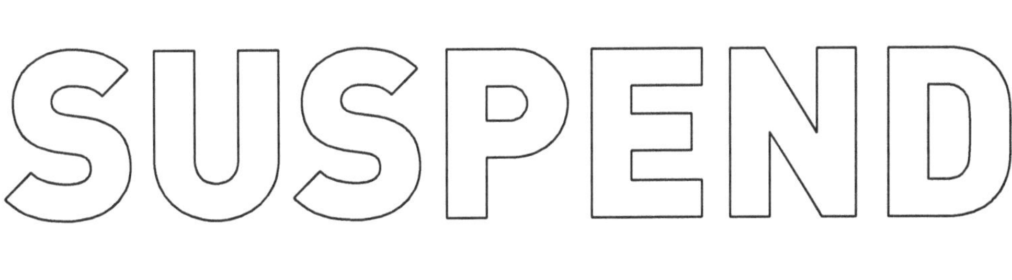
SUSPEND

Goals of Dance

Dynamics - Quality of Movement - Introduction to Suspend

Define the word **suspend**:

____

____

Discuss the quality of movement and give examples of suspended movement.

____

____

____

Let's Move: Explore suspended movement in the dance space.

Notes

____

____

____

____

____

Goals of Dance: Technique/Practice

Teachers will create a combination that uses **suspended** movement.
Students will write the combination in the box below.

Music for combination: ___________________________________

Name of the artist/musician: ______________________________

Theme of combination: ___________________________________

Suspend Combination

Combination Notes

Teachers will discuss movement details in the **suspended movement** combination. Students will write notes in the space provided below.

Dance Vocabulary Words

Please write the dance vocabulary words used in the combination and define if needed.

Class Notes and Review Sheet

Review the combination and write your notes.

Continue your practice.

List **three** notes you will continue to work on and practice.

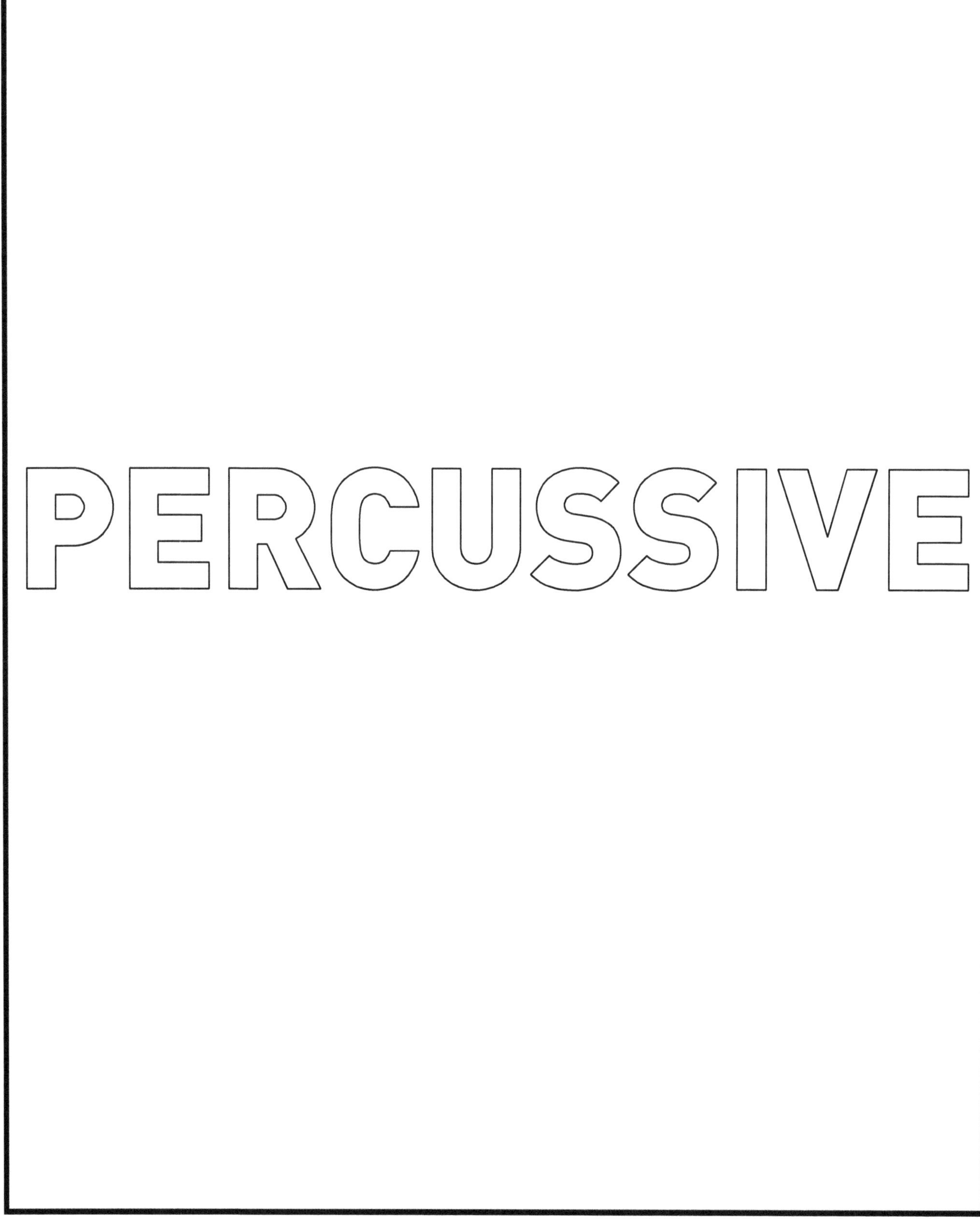
PERCUSSIVE

Goals of Dance

Dynamics - Quality of Movement - Introduction to Percussive

Define the word **percussive**:

Discuss the quality of movement and give examples of percussive movement.
How is percussive different from suspended movement?

Let's Move: Explore percussive movement in the dance space.

Notes

Goals of Dance: Technique/Practice

Teachers will create a combination that uses **percussive** movement.
Students will write the combination in the box below.

Music for combination: ___________________________________

Name of the artist/musician: ________________________________

Theme of combination: ___________________________________

Percussive Combination

Combination Notes

Teachers will discuss movement details in the **percussive movement** combination. Students will write notes in the space provided below.

Dance Vocabulary Words

Please write the dance vocabulary words used in the combination and define if needed.

Class Notes and Review Sheet

Review the combination and write your notes.

Continue your practice.

List **three** notes you will continue to work on and practice.

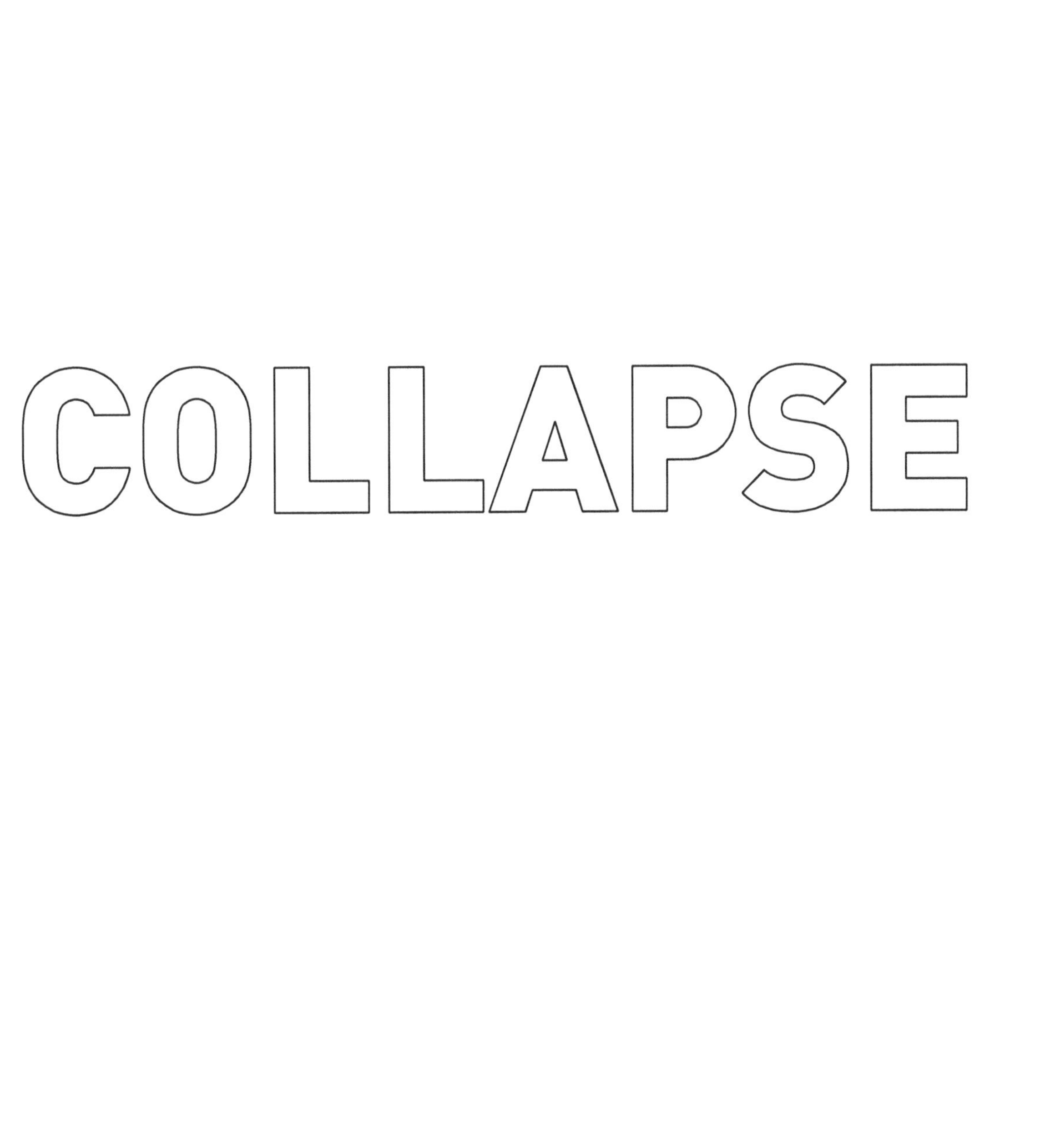
COLLAPSE

Goals of Dance

Dynamics - Quality of Movement - Introduction to Collapse

Define the word **collapse**:

____

____

Discuss the quality of movement and give examples of collapsed movement.
How is collapsed movement different from percussive?

____

____

____

Let's Move: Explore collapsed movement in the dance space.

Notes

____

____

____

____

____

____

Goals of Dance: Technique/Practice

Teachers will create a combination that uses **collapsed** movement.
Students will write the combination in the box below.

Music for combination: ____

Name of the artist/musician: ____________________________________

Theme of combination: ____

Collapsed Combination

Combination Notes

Teachers will discuss movement details in the **collapsed movement** combination. Students will write notes in the space provided below.

Dance Vocabulary Words

Please write the dance vocabulary words used in the combination and define if needed.

Class Notes and Review Sheet

Review the combination and write your notes.

____

____

____

____

____

____

____

Continue your practice.

List **three** notes you will continue to work on and practice.

____

____

____

____

SMOOTH

Goals of Dance

Dynamics - Quality of Movement - Introduction to Smooth

Define the word **smooth**:

____

____

Discuss the quality of movement and give examples of smooth movement.
How is this movement different from collapse?

____

____

____

Let's Move: Explore smooth movement in the dance space.

Notes

____

____

____

____

____

Goals of Dance: Technique/Practice

Teachers will create a combination that uses **smooth** movement.
Students will write the combination in the box below.

Music for combination: ______________________________

Name of the artist/musician: ______________________________

Theme of combination: ______________________________

Smooth Combination

Combination Notes

Teachers will discuss movement details in the **smooth movement** combination. Students will write notes in the space provided below.

Dance Vocabulary Words

Please write the dance vocabulary words used in the combination and define if needed.

Class Notes and Review Sheet

Review the combination and write your notes.

____

____

____

____

____

____

____

Continue your practice.

List **three** notes you will continue to work on and practice.

____

____

____

____

Goals of Dance

Dynamics - Quality of Movement

Select one dynamic and circle:

SUSPEND COLLAPSE PERCUSSIVE SMOOTH

Create an 8-count combination, using the dynamic selected.
Option: Create a 16-count combination, using the dynamic selected.

Practice your combination. Write the combination in the box below.

Videotape your combination with an electronic device and review the notes. If students do not have an electronic device, students can work with their teacher or a partner.

Write notes (things you need to work on) in the space provided below.

____

____

____

____

____

____

Review the notes observed in the video.
Practice your notes and make the corrections.

List **three** things you will continue to work on and practice:

____

____

____

____

____

____

SKILLS PRACTICE/PERFORMANCE- INDIVIDUAL ASSESSMENT

Name: ______________________________ Date: ________________

Name of the skill or combination: ______________________________

Rate your practice skills or combination in the following categories.
Circle the number or check the box.

CATEGORY	Excellent	Very Good	Average	Needs Work	SCORE
Dancing overall; execution of movement	5	4	3	2	______
Energy in movement	5	4	3	2	______
Applying all the choreographic notes	5	4	3	2	______
FILL IN THE CATEGORY/CREATE YOUR OWN CATEGORY:	5	4	3	2	______

TOTAL SCORE: ______

SCORE RUBRIC TOTAL SCORE _____

Circle your total score below

Excellent	Good	Average	Needs Work
20 - 17	16 - 13	12 - 9	8 - Below

Please explain your individual score overall.
Which category was your greatest success? Why?

___

___

___

Which category do you feel needs the most improvement? Why?

___

___

___

What can you do to prepare for the next practice skills assessment or performance? Explain in detail.

___

___

___

MUSICALITY IN MOVEMENT

Goals of Dance
Musicality in Movement Checklist

In this lesson students will.

_____ Define musicality.

_____ Explore different styles of music.

_____ Observe movement.

_____ Write notes on skills learned.

_____ Create movement, learn combinations.

_____ Assess skills learned.

_____ Other - Students and teachers can include additional goals below.

____

____

____

Goals of Dance

Introduction to Musicality in Movement

Music is one important part of the dance class and choreography. There are many different forms and styles of music. Finding the appropriate music for the dance class and choreography inspires creativity in movement. Some examples of music in a dance class include recorded, instrumental, and live music such as drums or bells. When dancers find the appropriate music, the dance comes alive.

Define the word below.

What is **MUSICALITY?**

____

____

____

Why is musicality important for dance and choreography?

____

____

____

What would a dance look like without music? Can a dancer perform without music?

____

____

____

Goals of Dance

Listen and Practice Worksheet 1: Musicality

Teachers and students will listen to different pieces of music and discuss the different qualities. Students can explore the different ways to move to the music and write notes below.

Name/description of music	Explore/describe your movement

Teachers will create a combination that demonstrates the **musicality** described above. Students will write combination in the box below.

Combination Notes

Teachers will discuss movement details in the **musicality** combination.
Students will write notes in the space provided below.

Goals of Dance
Listening and Practice Worksheet 2: Musicality

Teachers and students will listen to different pieces of music and discuss the different qualities. Students can explore the different ways to move to the music and write notes below.

Name/description of music	Explore/describe your movement

Teachers will create a combination that demonstrates the **musicality** described above. Students will write combination in the box below.

Combination Notes

Teachers will discuss movement details in the **musicality** combination.
Students will write notes in the space provided below.

Goals of Dance – Continued Study

Musicality in Movement Vocabulary 1

Teachers will discuss, define, and connect music vocabulary to their classroom or dance studio setting.

Define the following words. Think about how the words relate to the dance space. Also think about why the vocabulary is important to help the dancer gain success.

Adagio, Allegro

Rhythm, Beat

Tempo

Accent

Goals of Dance - Continued Study
Musicality in Movement Vocabulary 2

Select the music vocabulary appropriate for your dance studio or classroom setting.
List the words below and define the music vocabulary.

Think about how the words relate to the dance space.
Also think about why the vocabulary is important to help the dancer gain success.

Word Search: Musicality in Movement

Musicality	Rhythm	Accent	Beat
Polyrhythmic	Speed	Adagio	Tempo
Instruments	Allegro	Pulse	Sound

P	U	L	S	E	T	H	I	G	Y	S	D	V
D	S	T	N	E	M	U	R	T	S	N	I	A
H	R	J	M	T	E	C	I	W	X	O	D	L
S	E	P	R	N	B	L	A	G	M	N	E	L
O	O	A	Y	E	A	R	D	N	H	T	E	E
U	L	S	D	C	C	B	A	L	T	R	P	G
N	U	W	I	C	E	D	G	U	Y	O	S	R
D	O	S	E	A	E	N	I	D	H	L	N	O
E	U	S	T	P	E	L	O	I	R	E	D	N
M	P	O	L	Y	R	H	Y	T	H	M	I	C

Goals of Dance

Musicality Practice Choreography

Students will select a style or piece of music from the examples practiced in class.

Style of Music: ______________________________________

Create a combination and write the combination in the box below.

Describe the movement in your combination. Is it fast, slow, or a combination of both? Does the combination include different movement dynamics learned in this workbook?

____

____

____

Give your combination a title: ________________________________

Students will videotape their combination with an electronic device.

Option: If students do not have an electronic device, students can work with their teacher or a partner.

Observe the combination.

Students will then write notes and things they need to continue to work on in the space provided below.

____

____

____

____

____

____

____

____

____

____

____

____

____

SKILLS PRACTICE/PERFORMANCE- INDIVIDUAL ASSESSMENT

Name: ______________________________ Date: ________________

Name of the skill or combination: ________________________________

Rate your practice skills or combination in the following categories.
Circle the number or check the box.

CATEGORY	Excellent	Very Good	Average	Needs Work	**SCORE**
Dancing overall; execution of movement	5	4	3	2	________
Energy in movement	5	4	3	2	________
Applying all the choreographic notes	5	4	3	2	________
FILL IN THE CATEGORY/CREATE YOUR OWN CATEGORY:	5	4	3	2	________

TOTAL SCORE: ________

SCORE RUBRIC TOTAL SCORE _______

Circle your total score below

Excellent	Good	Average	Needs Work
20 - 17	16 - 13	12 - 9	8 - Below

Please explain your individual score overall.
Which category was your greatest success? Why?

____

____

____

Which category do you feel needs the most improvement? Why?

____

____

____

What can you do to prepare for the next practice skills assessment or performance?
Explain in detail.

____

____

____

ASSESSMENTS AND RESOURCES

Dance Corrections and Notes Worksheet

Today, I am working on:

____

____

Dance Class Corrections/Notes

1.

2.

3.

4.

5.

Today, after practicing dance technique/skills, I learned:

____

____

____

Dance Corrections/Notes Worksheet (Technique)

Name: ______________________________ Date: ______________

Success Corner! Great Job!

I need to continue to work on:

Practice Continued (Detailed Combination/Information)

My homework assignment is:

____

____

Homework Assignment Due Date: ______________________________

Upcoming Assessment(s), Other: ______________________________

Goals of Dance – Vocabulary Sheet

Today we are working on ____.

Select the vocabulary appropriate for your dance studio or classroom setting.
List the words below and define the vocabulary in the boxes provided.

Think about how the words relate to the dance space.

Also think about why the vocabulary is important to help the dancer gain success.

____

____

____

____

Dance Skills Practice Journal Worksheet A

Students will practice, write, and reflect on skills learned.

Name: ______________________________ Date: _______________

Today, I am working on:

____

____

BEFORE YOU PRACTICE: List **one** goal.
What do you want to achieve during your practice session?

____

****PRACTICE** *the movement or dance combination for 5-10 minutes. Use an electronic device to videotape your practice or have someone observe your practice and give you notes. Write the notes and things you need to work on below.*

NOTES: Please write your practice notes in detail below.

1. ____

2. ____

3. ____

RESULT: Did you achieve your goal? Answer in detail.

____

____

WEEKLY DANCE GOALS AND PRACTICE LOG

	MON	TUES	WED	THURS	FRI
Date:					
Check/Practice Completed:					

Goal for the week: ______________________________________

Write your daily notes below.

MONDAY ______________________________________

____

____

TUESDAY ______________________________________

____

____

WEDNESDAY ______________________________________

____

____

THURSDAY ____

____

____

FRIDAY ____

____

____

Did you achieve your weekly goal? ______________________________

I will continue to work on:

____

____

____

____

____

Dance Skills Practice Journal Worksheet B

Students will practice, write, and reflect on skills learned.

Name: ______________________________

Date: ______________________________

Today, I am working on:

____

____

BEFORE YOU PRACTICE: List **one** goal. What do you want to achieve during your practice session? Why is this goal important to you?

____

> ****PRACTICE** *the movement or combination for 5-10 minutes. Use an electronic device to videotape your practice or have someone observe your practice and give you notes. Write the notes and things you need to work on in the space provided below.*

PRACTICE NOTES: Please write your practice notes in detail below:

1. ____
2. ____
3. ____
4. ____
5. ____

RESULT: Did you achieve your goal? Answer in detail.

REFLECTION: How are you going to use the information learned during the practice in your dance classes?

WRITING: Dance Poem

Students will write an acrostic poem and create movement.
The title of the poem is dance.

D ______________________________

A ______________________________

N ______________________________

C ______________________________

E ______________________________

ABOUT THE AUTHOR

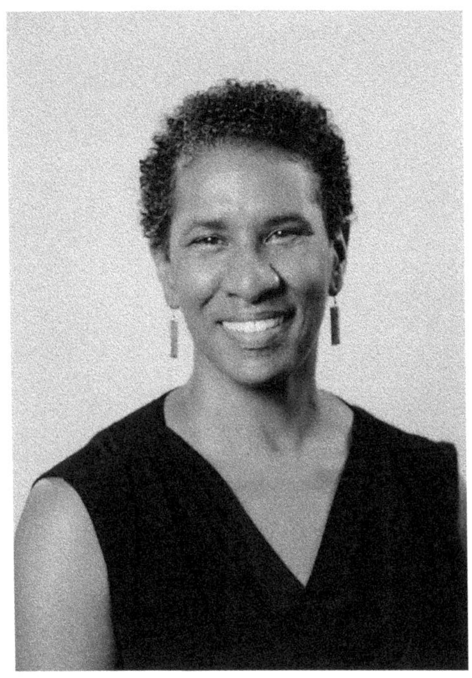

Nealya Brunson is currently a dance director and teacher in central Florida. She has dedicated over 20 years to educating students in dance and the arts. Her contributions to the success of her students have resulted in them receiving multiple college acceptances as well as scholarships. Her middle and high school students have also gone to participate in the Florida Dance Performance Assessment, receiving superior and excellent ratings in the areas of Dance Technique and Performance.

Over the years, Ms. Brunson has taught many students who have demonstrated outstanding achievements and have become professional dancers, artists, teachers, and choreographers, nationally and internationally.

Ms. Brunson worked as a dance program coordinator, choreographing dance performances for many dance and theater programs while also serving as a dance adjudicator in several public schools, universities, and performing arts centers, primarily in the state of Florida.

Ms. Brunson's training in dance began in St. Petersburg, Florida at B.J.'s School of Dance, under the direction of Barbara Hodges. She continued to study dance in Pinellas County School for the Arts at Gibbs High School, as well as St. Petersburg College, CoMotion Dance Theater. Ms. Brunson received a Bachelor of Fine Arts in Dance from the University of Florida, New World School of the Arts in Miami, Florida, under the direction of Daniel Lewis. She also received a Master of Arts in Dance from the American University in Washington, D.C. under the direction of Dr. Niama Prevots.

Ms. Brunson enjoys teaching and studying dance, movement, and alignment, which are a major component of her modern dance classes. She created this book to serve as a primary resource for teachers looking to incorporate reading, writing, and creative movement into their own unique classroom or studio setting. The lessons in this book and her other publications will enhance student learning and help students practice the goals of dance and technique, with more workbooks on the way.

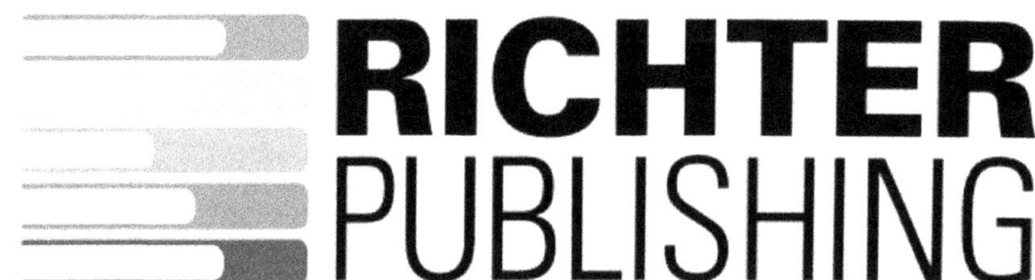
RICHTER
PUBLISHING

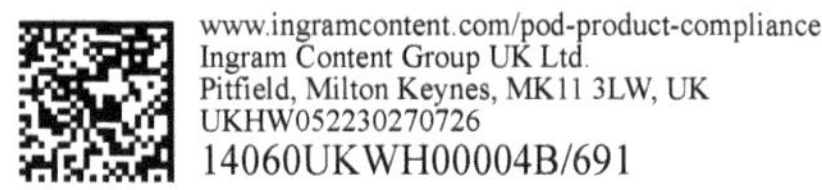
www.ingramcontent.com/pod-product-compliance
Ingram Content Group UK Ltd.
Pitfield, Milton Keynes, MK11 3LW, UK
UKHW052230270726
14060UKWH00004B/691

9 781954 094994